PET DOCTOR

...

BY **Harriet Langsam Sobol**

PHOTOGRAPHS BY **Patricia Agre**

G. P. Putnam's Sons

NEW YORK

Acknowledgments
Special thanks to Ellen Anders, Dr. Nicholas Di Russo,
Dr. William Lewit, Liz Mark and Dr. Michael Wolland.

Library of Congress Cataloging-in-Publication Data
Sobol, Harriet Langsam.   Pet doctor.
Summary: Follows Dr. Salm, a veterinarian,
as he treats cats, dogs, rabbits, birds, and other
pets, providing check-ups, immunizations, and
answers to questions about animal behavior.
1. Veterinarians—Juvenile literature.   2. Veteri-
nary medicine—Juvenile literature.   3. Pets—
Diseases—Juvenile literature.   4. Salm, Herbert—
Juvenile literature.   5. Veterinarians—United States—
Biography—Juvenile literature.   [1. Veterinarians.
2. Veterinary medicine.   3. Occupations.   4. Salm,
Herbert]   I. Agre, Patricia, ill. II. Title.
SF756.S63   1988   636.089′092′4   87-25881
ISBN 0-399-21533-6

636
S   c. 1   13.95   9/92

To Dr. Herbert Salm, Maggie Cholet,
Margaret Jurmak and Sigi Allen

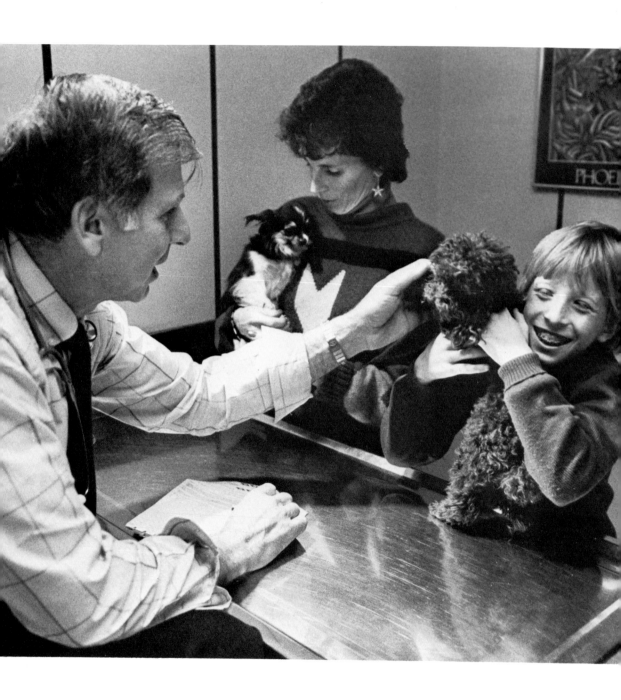

Dr. Herbert Salm is a veterinarian, a doctor who cares for animals. He spends most of his time looking after dogs and cats, but he also sees rabbits, turtles, birds, snakes, gerbils and other small pets. Veterinarians care for the health of animals in the same way that doctors care for the health of people.

Dr. Salm has an office where people bring their pets for checkups and for treatment if they are sick or hurt. The office has a waiting room with chairs, a receptionist's desk, an examining room, a treatment room, an X-ray room, a surgical room, a grooming room, a room with cages for sick animals, and a room for boarding animals that are being looked after while their owners are away.

Several trained technicians help Dr. Salm treat and examine the animals. They also develop X rays and run laboratory tests. Kennel workers keep the animal cages clean so that the sick animals and the boarding animals will feel clean and comfortable. A receptionist makes appointments and sends out bills.

When Dr. Salm was a little boy he lived on a dairy farm. He spent much of his time working with the cows and chickens and other farm animals. When he grew up he decided that he wanted to be a veterinarian, and take care of pets.

Veterinary students study their profession for four years after college. Many spend a year or more working at an animal hospital after they graduate from veterinary school to get additional experience before opening up a practice of their own.

Pet owners make appointments ahead of time with Dr. Salm unless there is an emergency. Dr. Salm will see a pet immediately if it is seriously ill or hurt.

Dr. Salm's patients and their owners wait for their appointments in the waiting room of his animal hospital. Often there are several animals in the waiting room at once. Dr. Salm likes owners to bring dogs on leashes and cats and birds in carriers. If they are allowed to run loose, there might be a fight!

An important part of Dr. Salm's work is preventive medicine—preventing an animal from getting ill. He keeps a health record for each patient with the animal's health history. He gives animals shots to protect them against certain diseases, just as doctors give children injections to protect them from tetanus, whooping cough, and measles. Some of the diseases that shots can prevent in animals are rabies, distemper, and cat leukemia. These shots are called *immunizations*. The medicine that is injected into the animal to protect it from disease is called a *vaccine*.

Many pet owners take their puppies and kittens to the veterinarian for routine checkups and immunizations just as parents take their children to

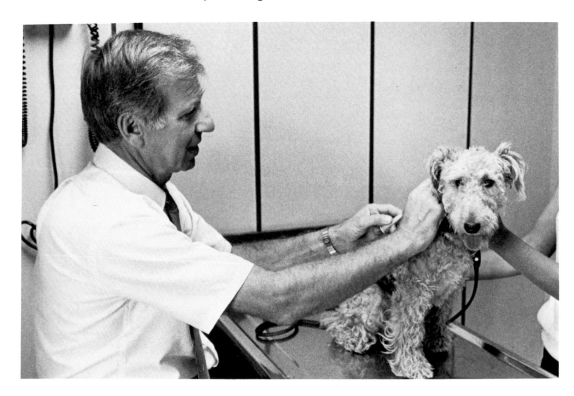

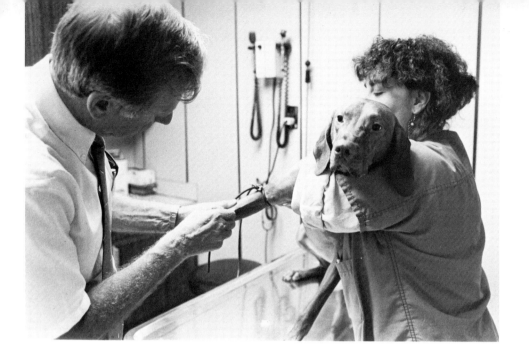

pediatricians. Some diseases, like rabies, can be passed from animals to human beings, so immunizing pets also protects the people with whom they come into contact. If they are not immunized, dogs and cats can catch rabies from being bitten by a rabid animal.

A new pet should be taken to the veterinarian right away so the doctor can check the animal's health. When a pet is brought in for a checkup, Dr. Salm weighs it and listens to the animal's heart and lungs. He looks at its ears and teeth, checks its temperature, and looks for fleas. Cats have a blood test for feline leukemia and dogs have a blood test for heartworms. Dr. Salm also takes a stool specimen to check for worms.

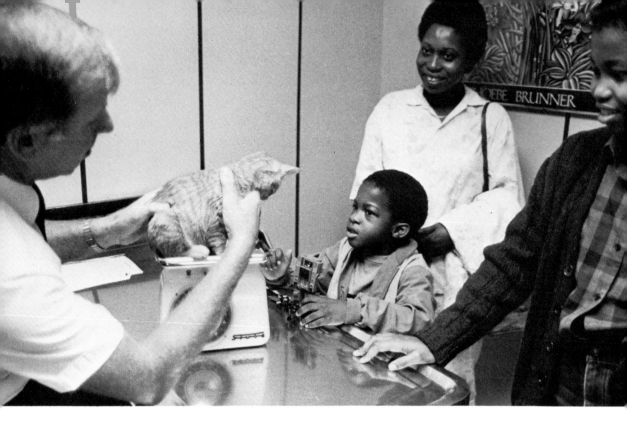

Goldie is the first pet the Owens family has ever owned.

"I love her," says Larry Owens.

"We all love her," says his sister.

While Dr. Salm is weighing the kitten, he asks the Owenses whether they plan to keep Goldie inside the house or let her go outside. If she goes outside she should be immunized against cat leukemia.

Dr. Salm also asks the Owenses whether they want Goldie to have kittens when she is old enough. If they don't, they are to bring Goldie back when she is six months old to be spayed. Spaying is an operation that prevents female animals from getting pregnant. While the animal is sleeping under general anesthesia, the veterinarian removes her ovaries and uterus.

Male dogs and cats can have their testicles removed to prevent them from making females pregnant. This surgery is called *altering*. Most dogs and cats can go home the day after they are spayed or altered.

Dr. Salm suggests to pet owners that they have their kittens and puppies spayed or altered. There are so many unwanted cats and dogs in the world that most veterinarians encourage people not to let their pets have litters unless they want to breed them.

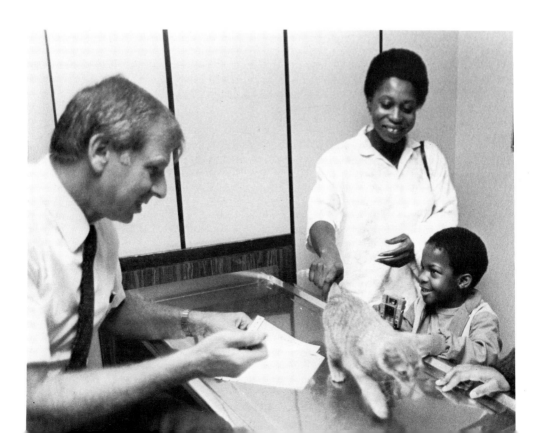

Dr. Salm advises pet owners about their animal's diet and exercise as well as behavior. He answers questions about housebreaking, chewing, and scratching. He may suggest a scratching post for a kitten so she doesn't scratch the furniture. He usually suggests that owners take their puppies for obedience training.

Sometimes owners have problems with their pets and they ask Dr. Salm about them. "Apollo scratches himself all the time," a young woman says.

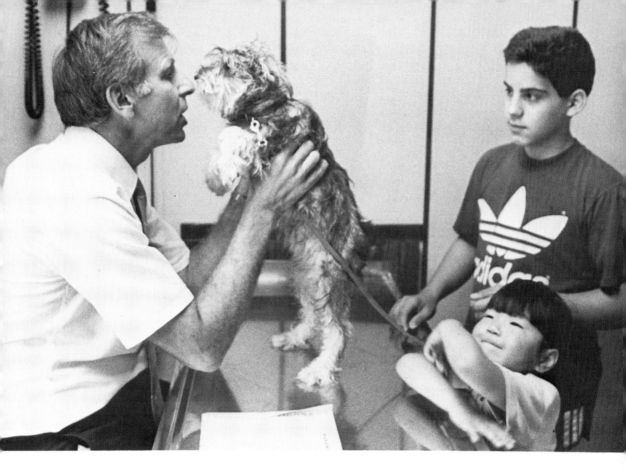

Dr. Salm tells her that Apollo has fleas. "Why don't you leave him for a flea bath. That should make him feel better for a while, but if he keeps going outside in the warm weather, he might get fleas again."

Dr. Salm's next patient is a puppy. Her owner complains, "Ethel chews on everyone's shoes."

Dr. Salm suggests to Ethel's owner, "Ethel is just a puppy. Say 'No,' to her whenever you catch her chewing, and she'll outgrow it."

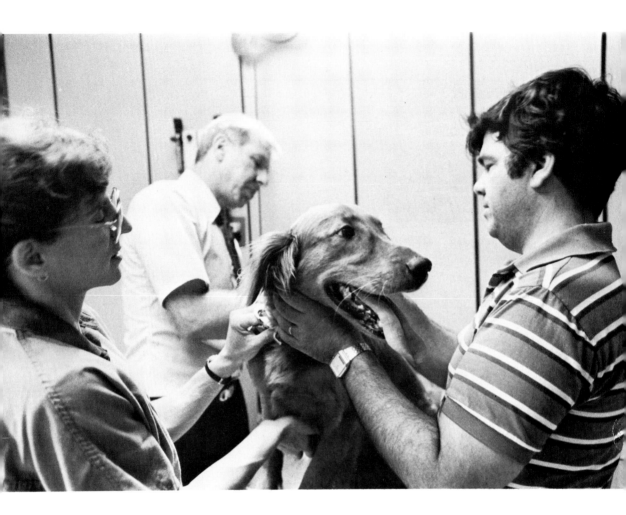

Smokey, a golden retriever, jumps up on people when they come into the house. Dr. Salm tells Smokey's owner, "I think you should take Smokey to obedience school."

Dr. Salm understands animal behavior and has cared for so many animals that he is able to give good advice to pet owners.

Dr. Salm tells the owner of Shep, a matted bearded collie, "Shep must be groomed professionally. Her hair's all matted, especially on the paws."

Most of the animals that come to Dr. Salm's animal hospital are healthy and come for routine care. Some pets are old and suffer from the same kind of problems that bother old people. Their owners love them and feel very sad when they are sick.

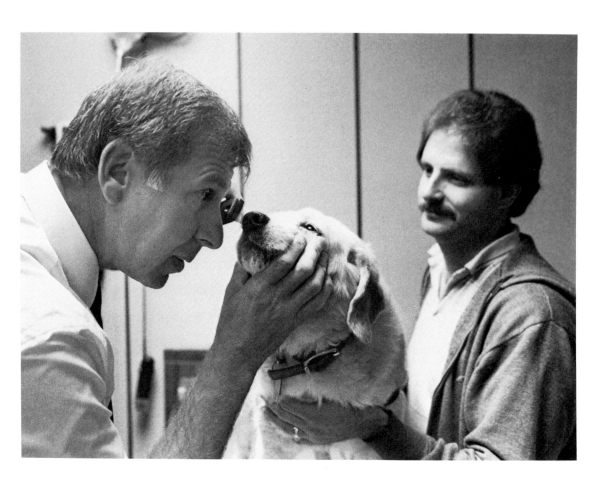

Pal is fourteen years old and he doesn't see very well anymore. Pal has lived with the Greenes since before Joey Greene was born. Joey is two years old now and loves Pal very much. Poor Pal has arthritis, so it's hard for him to go up and down stairs. Dr. Salm explains that Pal is getting old and things are getting harder for him. He prescribes aspirin for the arthritis. Dr. Salm checks Pal's teeth before he lifts Pal off the examining table.

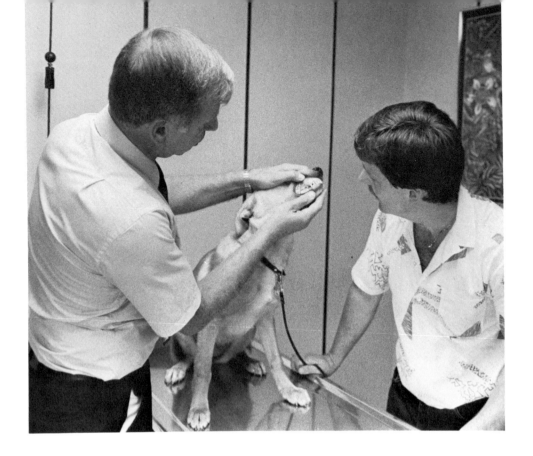

Animals' teeth need care just as people's teeth do. Dr. Salm checks his patients' teeth when they come in for a visit. If the teeth need cleaning, he asks the owner to make a special appointment. At that time Dr. Salm gives the animal a general anesthetic so it will stay still while its teeth are being cleaned.

Mrs. Abbot brings her two cats into the examining room. Meanwhile two dogs that belong to the Burke family are in the waiting room. Some people have two pets so the animals can keep each other company.

Dr. Salm takes care of all kinds of cats and dogs—
big dogs, little dogs, Siamese cats, and domestic
cats.

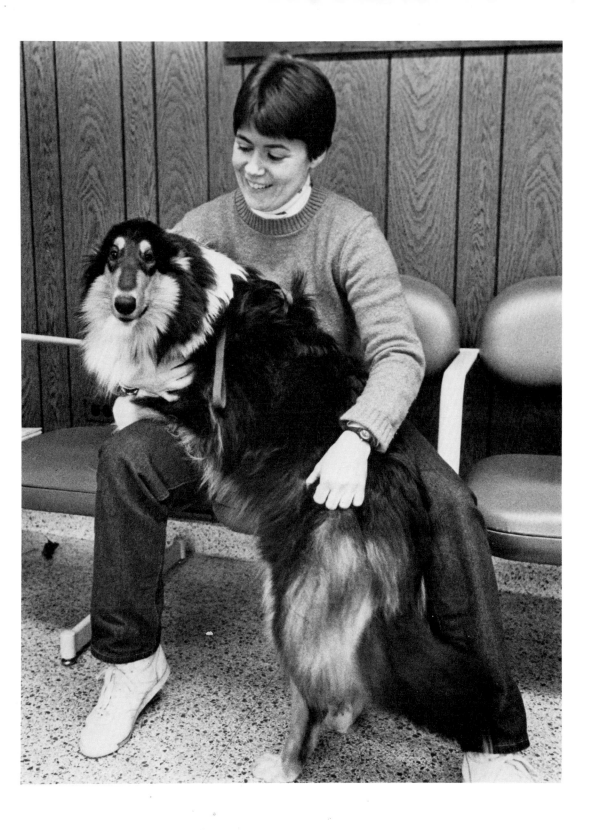

Occasionally he has small pets as patients. A white rat may have hurt his leg on an exercise wheel; a bird may have fallen from a tree.

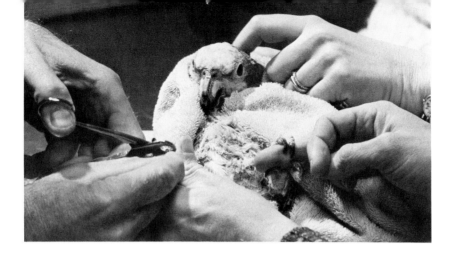

Captain, a parrot, has been coming to Dr. Salm for many years to have his claws trimmed. Captain doesn't like to be held down. Dr. Salm's assistants wrap him in a towel so Captain won't struggle while Dr. Salm clips his claws. As soon as he is finished clipping the claws, the assistants release Captain so he can go to the safety of his owner's hand.

Fluffy is being dropped off to be spayed. Dr. Salm instructs her owner to call later in the day to find out how she is and when she will be ready to go home. About a week after Fluffy goes home, she will have to come back to Dr. Salm to have her stitches out.

Sometimes Dr. Salm has to operate on animals to make them better. Candy was hit by a car. Her owner was taking her for a walk when the leash broke. Candy ran away and darted across a large street. Fortunately, her only injury was a broken leg. Dr. Salm gave her anesthesia so she wouldn't feel any pain. While Candy was sleeping, Dr. Salm set her leg and put it in a cast. Today is the day for the cast to come off. Candy will be so pleased to be rid of the cast.

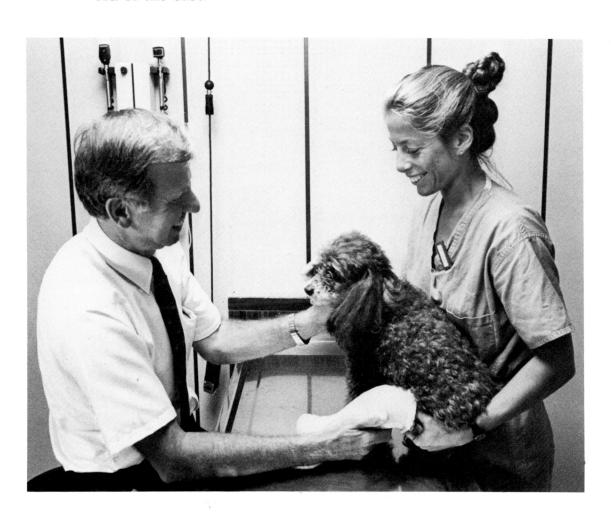

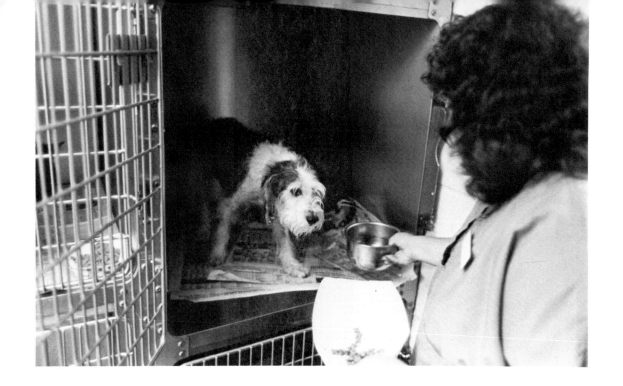

In back of his examining room, Dr. Salm has large animal cages for sick animals or animals who have had surgery. Fluffy will rest in a cage after her spaying until she goes back to her owner. When Candy had her leg set, she stayed in a cage until she was well enough to go home. Dr. Salm's helpers keep the cages clean and talk to the animals so they will feel cared for and not miss their owners and homes too much.

In another room there are cages for animals that are being boarded. People who go away and have no one at home to look after their pets bring them to Dr. Salm because they know he will care for them well. The pet owners pay Dr. Salm a boarding fee.

Once in a while Dr. Salm sees a very sick animal. Flopsy is a flop-eared rabbit. Dr. Salm has cared for her for several years. Flopsy has been sick before but she has always gotten better. She has never been this sick. Poor Flopsy is so sick now that she may not get well. An assistant gently takes Flopsy out of her carrier. Dr. Salm tells her owner that he will keep her overnight so he can give her fluid through a needle he will put under her skin. "You can call me in the morning and see how she is, but I don't think she's going to get better. She's an old rabbit and she probably won't live very long. The kindest thing may be to put her to sleep."

When Dr. Salm says that it would be kinder to "put Flopsy to sleep," he means that sometimes it is kinder to help an animal to die peacefully and without pain when it cannot live any longer without suffering.

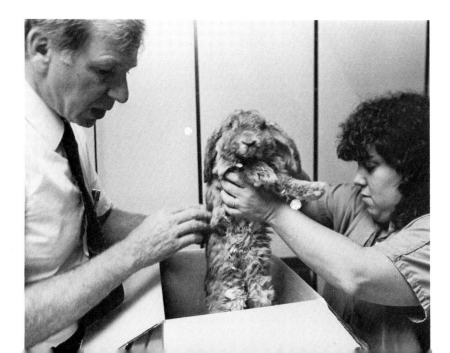

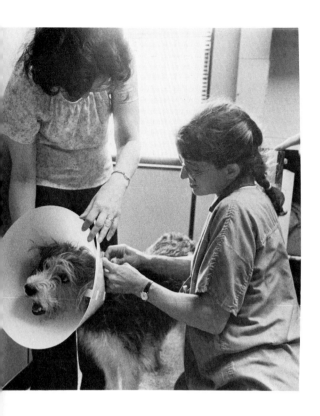

A week ago Korky had an infection on her side. Dr. Salm cleaned it and put medicine on it but Korky kept licking it. Dr. Salm put a plastic collar around Korky's neck so she wouldn't lick or scratch the wound.

Samantha has a high fever. She has been in a fight with a raccoon and has a bad abscess on her leg. Dr. Salm says to her owner, "I think I'd better keep her for a few days so I can give her antibiotics. Call me in the morning and see how she's doing."

Not all veterinarians see pets in an office. Some veterinarians have vans that are outfitted inside like animal hospitals. These veterinarians bring their skills to people who are not able to leave their homes.

Veterinarians help to keep pets healthy in the same way doctors keep people healthy. They try to prevent animals from becoming ill and treat them if they should get sick. Most of all, pets need loving care and attention from their owners.

DATE DUE